SUMMARY

"A long-lasting marriage is built by two people who believe in -and live by- the solemn promise they made."
- Darlene Schacht

The crazy thing about marriage is that most of us enter into this union by making a pledge that many of us do not understand and most of us have never really thought about. We know that the Marriage Vows are essential. But, we do not take the time to expound on them.

Establishing Glory 3: The Marriage Handbook takes a deep dive into the vows that we exchange with our spouse on our special day.

As a follow-up to the Praise and Worship Handbook and the

Relationship Handbook, Best-Selling Author - Jackie Smith, Jr. takes an honest and unfiltered look into the challenges and achievements that marriage can present us.

So, whether you've been married for 90 years, or you're planning to get married one day, "Establishing Glory 3: The Marriage Handbook" is for YOU!

ESTABLISHING GLORY 3

ESTABLISHING GLORY 3

The Marriage Handbook

JACKIE SMITH, JR.

Copyright © 2019 J Merrill Publishing, Inc.

All rights reserved. No part of this publication may be reproduced, distributed, or transmitted in any form or by any means, including photocopying, recording, or other electronic or mechanical methods, without the prior written permission of the publisher, except in the case of brief quotations embodied in critical reviews and certain other noncommercial uses permitted by copyright law. For permission requests, write to the publisher, addressed "Attention: Permissions Coordinator," at the address below.

ISBN: 978-1-950719-15-0 (Hardback)
ISBN: 978-1-950719-13-6 (Paperback)
ISBN: 978-1-950719-14-3 (eBook)

Any references to historical events, real people, or real places are used fictitiously. Names, characters, and places are products of the author's imagination.

FIRST printing edition 2019.

J Merrill Publishing, Inc.
434 Hillpine Drive
Columbus, OH 43207

www.JMerrillPublishingInc.com

I'd like to dedicate this book, first and foremost, to God. This would not have been possible without His inspiration, leadership, and guidance.

And to my wife: Life wouldn't be the same without you. I love you to life!

CONTENTS

Preface	xi
1. I Take Thee To Be My Wedded	1
2. To Have And To Hold	9
3. From This Day Forward	21
4. For Better, For Worse	33
5. For Richer, For Poorer: Beyond Money	45
6. In Sickness and in Health: A Reflection on Marriage Vows	61
7. To Love and To Cherish	75
8. Till Death Do Us Part	93
9. According To God's Holy Ordinance	111
10. And Thereto I Pledge Myself To You	129
Endnotes	141
About the Author	143
Also by Jackie Smith, Jr.	145

PREFACE

When I first began to ponder the Marriage Handbook, I was looking at life retrospectively and considering all the ways I had been a good husband. I started compiling a list of the many disagreements we've had, showing how she was wrong, and I was right. Let me tell you, I have some doozies.

The crazy part about examining your life is that the longer the spotlight shines inward, the more flaws and imperfections within you are revealed. As I delved into the bullet points of my notes, I saw that there were moments when I was entirely right, and my feelings and

PREFACE

point of view were justified. But there were also moments when I was being unreasonable and, quite honestly, an idiot.

There are so many self-help books out there that you may ask, "Who needs another one?" But I'm not writing this book for you; I'm writing it for me.

The deeper my introspective search went, the more I found that many of the lessons I failed today were like those I failed yesterday. In speaking with others, I found they are failing many of the same lessons repeatedly, as well.

To give a brief history, I married on August 15, 1994. So, as of today (June 20, 2019), I have been married for twenty-four years, ten months, and five days. The problem is that I've been divorced twice since then and am currently in my third marriage.

My first marriage lasted just over one year; my second, over twenty-one years. My current wife and I are celebrating one year, seven months, and nine days—but who's counting?

In these past twenty-four years, I have been part of two blended families, been a father to almost forty children, experienced five failed or miscarried pregnancies, been laid off three times, owned four businesses, lost my mother and grandmother, attempted suicide, and become an author-publisher, to name a few things. Trust me, the stories I will share will genuinely cause you to think long and hard about this thing called "marriage."

One key to marriage is balance. When I began to pen this manuscript, I knew we needed to start with this question: "Where do we find this balance?"

The answer was simple: The key to balance in marriage starts at the altar. It begins with the commitment we voice to one another in our vows. So, we're going to take an in-depth look at these vows and understand the power that these simple words hold, not only for our lives but also for everyone connected to us.

Let's get started.

I

I TAKE THEE TO BE MY WEDDED

When it comes to critical points in the timeline of relationships that lead to marriage, three come to mind: the proposal, the vows, and the honeymoon.

From a man's perspective, the proposal is important because this is when he officially turns in his "Player's Card." He has made a conscious decision to be with this one woman for the rest of his life and is willing to make this commitment legal.

From a woman's perspective, this special moment occurs when her player's card is played, and she decides to be with this one man for the rest of her life, willing to make this legal commitment. (Sounds familiar, doesn't it?)

What makes this moment critical is not merely the investment in the ring, preparing the "perfect moment," getting down on one knee, or "popping the question." This moment is monumental because he declares that no one else matters except his chosen one.

I could be mistaken, but for the future bride, the monumental moment is likely centered more on the responses to the proposal and the subsequent announcement. The bent knee, the awaited question, and even the ring give her a warm and exciting sense of being special and valued. The announcement to family and friends adds to her sense of worth.

For many men, this is a moment of gravity, one of the most staggering changes they will ever make in their lives. There can be a certain sense of hesitation, if only for a moment or two. Alternatively, this hesitation might come after the proposal, when he experiences a maze of thoughts about the enormity of everything, intertwined with anticipation of the new adventure ahead.

Some men decide to propose only after seriously pondering whom they want to spend their lives with. Before settling on "the one," both men and women have spent time with others, each special in their unique ways. Admittedly, some attractions can be relatively shallow: one might be a better kisser, another looks particularly good in jeans, his complexion is rugged, or her eyes are captivating.

On the other hand, more serious matters require consideration: health issues, children in the package, adult children lingering, work ethic observed, and distance as a factor. Everything about the potential life mate is part of the picture.

Then arise the matters of disagreements in those relationships. Every couple has them, but how intense do the conflicts become? What kinds of issues ignite these conflicts? How long do these disputes last?

One man had two teenage boys, and the special woman in his life had two as well. She claimed he was too soft on his boys, raising them to be weak. Conversely, he felt her boys were too independent because she worked excessively. This disagreement flared up repeatedly, begging many questions.

Another example: both individuals have children but live on opposite sides of the same city. As is the woman, the man is content with his children's progress in their respective schools. Each child has good grades and many friends. She insists they will live on her side of town when they combine households, even though they never discussed marriage. He counters that since he already owns a house, they can merge families there. Neither would budge, prioritizing their children. This discussion lasted weeks and sometimes escalated intensely.

Then there was the couple who worked in separate locations but for the same employer. They would FaceTime each other while preparing for work and while driving to and from work. They would email, text, and instant message each other throughout the workday. They would regularly have lunch together. Their issue arose when the man didn't want to spend time with the woman in the evenings. He figured they'd been together all day and wanted some space. She, however, wanted to spend those evenings together. This disagreement regarding "time spent" continued for several weeks, and this tension was more like a smoldering cigarette threatening to ignite a brush fire!

The point is, each person desires or enjoys something that makes the other uncomfortable. Finding a balance can be a significant challenge.

Here, the pronoun "I" becomes central. This single-letter word is perhaps the most powerful in the commitment ceremony and the entire relationship. Before we can commit, we must know who we truly are!

For men, this self-awareness is challenging. It's easy to focus on what the woman brings: her attributes, likes, needs, dislikes, and expendabilities. We quickly see others' greatness or flaws. However, turning that light onto ourselves is an entirely different matter.

The most significant lies we tell are to ourselves. We're aware of our shortcomings, which we often disregard or conceal. We know our strengths and emphasize them.

But if I don't know who I am, how can I comprehend what becoming a husband means? How can I lead a wife—and possibly a family—when I don't even know where I'm going, let alone how to get there? Should I just wing it, hoping and praying for a good life?

Is it practical to embark on this new journey with some lofty but vague notion of us being a power-couple like Jay-Z and Beyoncé or Alex Rodriguez and Jennifer Lopez, when I haven't taken the time to understand myself through God's guidance?

No, sir, and no, ma'am!

Self-discovery begins with "why" and ends with "what."

Men, ask yourselves why you love this woman and want to propose. Know yourselves well enough to understand what makes you the men you are.

Women, inquire what you see in this man that will make life a memorable journey. What character traits does he bring into the relationship that will help you grow and dream? Again, know yourself well enough to believe you can add value to his life.

Genuine self-assessment is even more crucial than focusing on the other person's attributes or flaws.

I often tell people that I recognize my shortcomings, admit my imperfections, and acknowledge that I can be challenging to deal with. While I can be loving, kind, and caring, I'm fully aware that I can also be a jerk—an understanding my wife shares and for which I've apologized more than once. This book isn't written because I'm a paragon of marital perfection. No, I'm writing this book because I've made mistakes in marriage and have been divorced twice. Our failings weren't solely "her fault."

Before diving into the institution of marriage, it's vital to understand that it starts with "me" and ends with "we."

After completing our self-assessments, we

are better positioned to establish mutual goals. What once were individual aspirations now transform into a partnership of purpose. Both parties should seek ways to collaborate in areas of strength and growth, as intentionally as they would for their own personal goals.

Marriage is a partnership. That's why we both utter the same vows.

2
TO HAVE AND TO HOLD

Did you know that...

- Every thirteen seconds, a divorce occurs in America.
- Nine divorces take place in the time it takes for a couple to recite their wedding vows (two minutes).
- Almost fifty percent of all marriages in the United States will end in divorce or separation.

Is this crazy information to attach to a book about marriage?

In reality, many people are infatuated with the idea of marriage rather than with the institution itself. When some individuals hear the term "institution," they might think of the film "One Flew Over the Cuckoo's Nest," starring Jack Nicholson. Given the statistics, it may appear marriage could be compared to mental health—hopefully more in jest than seriously.

However, when we enter marriage with eyes wide open, we stand a better chance of falling on the positive side of these statistics.

As I began contemplating this chapter, I realized I needed to define "have" and "hold." The more I pondered these simple words, the more expansive their meanings became.

TO HAVE

Here are a few definitions for "have":

- To hold or maintain as a possession, privilege, or entitlement.
- To feel an obligation with regard to.
- To experience, especially by submitting to, undergoing, or suffering.

Most often, when we use the word "have," we refer to the first definition related to possession. Upon taking our vows, we believe we now possess a spouse: "She is my wife" or "He is my husband." And to be fair, there's a level of truth to this perspective.

However, I'd like to shift the focus to the latter definition, emphasizing submission, undergoing experiences, and even enduring suffering. Using this framework, we are not the possessors in the marriage; instead, we are possessed—quite the opposite of the standard view.

Our entitlement mentality leads us to believe we've reached the pinnacle of relationship theory simply by getting married.

Singles' events are behind us; dating is over. We now expect invitations to events and socials for married couples. Our "player's cards" are turned in, and we think we're on the road to marital bliss. Unfortunately, this is far from the truth.

Take my daily routine, for example. I used to arrive at work at the same time every day. My mornings typically included grabbing coffee and a breakfast sandwich before heading to the elevator en route to my office. I would greet familiar faces in the elevator.

However, one morning, I wore my wedding ring and found only one woman in the elevator. Her reaction stunned me. After my usual greeting, she asked for my name and where I worked, claiming she'd never seen me before. This was odd because I'd ridden the elevator with her many times, even as recently as the day before. The sole difference was the presence of my ring.

Had my wedding ring veiled my persona? Had it rendered me faceless? Had its presence sent her some unspoken message?

Some believe that interacting with people

of different marital statuses is taboo—a single woman conversing with a married man must be scandalous. So, even if she engages him daily in elevator small talk, she should pretend not to see him. She should remain entirely detached.

In this specific example, the opposite seems to be true. The woman knowingly interacted with a married man. Did the ring on his finger open doors? Did his marital status function as a green light for a fleeting encounter with no commitment or longevity? Is this how extramarital relationships begin?

Should people of different marital statuses interact with each other?

Before addressing this question, let's examine another example.

A couple experiencing marital challenges sought advice from another couple who appeared to have a successful marriage. The time spent was mutually beneficial. However, the husband from the troubled marriage (Husband A) and the wife from the stable marriage (Wife B) struck up a friendship outside of the couples' therapy. Though nothing inappropriate occurred, Wife A grew suspicious.

This raises a new question: "Should married individuals engage with people of the opposite sex when their spouses aren't present?"

There are culturally and socially acceptable ways for individuals to interact. Conversely, some interactions are deemed inappropriate. For example, married people are considered out-of-bounds when maintaining friendships with people of the opposite sex, particularly when meeting or talking on the phone without their spouse.

The underlying theme remains consistent: the contrast between owning the marriage and being enslaved by it. In the institution of marriage, spouses choose to serve each other's welfare mutually, which demands effort.

Contrary to fairy-tale narratives, marriage is not about riding off into the sunset or living happily ever after. Instead, it is a conscious, purposeful commitment requiring a deliberate and sometimes grueling effort to achieve short-term, even daily, goals for a successful life together.

For example, one of my objectives is to make my wife smile daily through intentional actions. The ultimate goal is her smile. While it may seem rudimentary, life's complexities make a simple smile powerful. Although I am not always successful, failure does not deter my attempts the following day.

JACKIE SMITH, JR.

TO HOLD

Here are a few definitions for "hold":

- To grasp, carry, or support with one's arms or hands.
- To remain secure, intact, or in position without breaking or giving way.
- To keep or reserve for someone.

When we contemplate the phrase "to hold," we generally focus on the first definition: mutual support. But the concept extends beyond mere support.

During the dating phase, we gravitate toward the third definition—reserving or keeping for someone—as we anticipate life with our future spouse.

Upon exchanging rings, we commit to a role that we must maintain without fail—that of a husband or wife. Why? Because there are entities wishing to separate *"what God hath joined together,"* according to the King James Version of the Bible. The ironic aspect is that often, the enemy threatening the marriage is oneself.

As a survivor of two failed marriages, I understand we can sometimes be our own worst enemies in matrimony. Our habits can foster a climate of self-destruction that only divine intervention and a loving spouse can mitigate.

But what lies at the core of these destructive patterns? Why do they manifest?

How often have we heard or said, "I'm not used to this; we've only been married for [insert number of years]?" Or "I'm still learning; give me a chance."

I know a man who has been married for over thirty years and claims he is "still learning" how to cook. Every time he says this, I can't help but laugh. It's far from the truth. Everyone in his circle knows he will never learn to cook; it's simply not a priority for him. He lacks the requisite interest for change.

Once upon a time, his spouse would criticize him for not contributing to meal preparation. But then she recognized that he was willing to clear the table and wash dishes while he might not be cooking. His contribution differed from her expectations, but it was a contribution nonetheless.

We can perpetuate self-deceptions, convincing ourselves that "someday" we'll improve. Yet such delusions can spell the end of our marriages.

So, what other habits undermine our marriages?

One area I'm working on is effective communication with my spouse. At face value, you might question how sharing information can be destructive. Well, it's not the content of the information that's the issue—it's the misunderstanding it can cause.

For example, as an author and publisher, my office is in my home. On some days, my wife also works from home. However, sharing a physical space doesn't mean we are both "at home"; in reality, we are "at work."

Take today, for instance. Our grandchild is visiting. My wife reminded me that WE are babysitting, even though I had previously told her that today would be focused on work. So,

I found myself having to cease work: first for a breakfast she prepared (which was excellent, by the way), then for babysitting, and later for some paperwork she needed. Each interruption led to work stoppages. What's amusing is that she apologizes for each interruption.

The dilemma arises if I tell her I need space or insist she act like I'm not present. But if I vent through writing—as I'm doing now—I might also create tension. Bottling up emotions usually backfires, surfacing later in unrelated conversations. Failing to communicate isn't a "them" problem; it's a "me" problem.

And what does this have to do with "to hold"?

It boils down to feeling—and being—secure in our marriages. When we avoid frank discussions out of fear or discomfort, we forfeit moments of connection and security. We may be undermining our relationships and setting ourselves up for external temptations. Alternatively, pent-up hostilities can prevent us from sharing genuine concerns, further eroding the marital bond.

The truth is, the most significant moments a couple can share occur after we've made amends and hashed out our differences. It's time for "make-up sex." Can I get an Amen?

That's when we truly get to hold each other.

But seriously, many children have been conceived in the aftermath of life's storms. These moments are often among the most pivotal and foundational in our families.

To strengthen our marriages, we must learn how to hold them properly.

3
FROM THIS DAY FORWARD

Let's begin with a few definitions of the word "forward":

- In the direction that one is facing or traveling; toward the front.
- Onward so as to make progress; toward a successful conclusion.
- Toward the future; ahead in time.
- An attacking player in basketball, hockey, or other sports.
- Help to advance something; promote.

As we examine these definitions and explore how each applies to marriage vows, we'll gain a broader view of the phrase "from this day forward."

One of the first challenges is achieving clarity about our objectives in our new life as a couple. Beyond being faithful, and as the Bible tells us to "be fruitful and multiply," what is the purpose of marriage? What is our union's goal? Why are we doing this?

My question to couples is simple: after the honeymoon phase, why are we getting married, and what does the future genuinely hold for us as a union?

We've all known couples who chose to marry but ended up in divorce court. The reasons may vary, but one could be failing to establish shared objectives.

People often get so caught up in the emotional highs of marital bliss that they don't take the time to consider their plans and purposes for their life together.

The first definition above discusses the direction we are facing or traveling. Critical questions arise: Are you financially secure? Do you own a house? Do you have reliable transportation? Is your bank account balance more than one hundred dollars? Are you racking up overdraft fees? Is your employment stable? Can you support more than just yourself? If you fall short on these, how committed are you to achieving these objectives?

Regrettably, I learned poor money management from my parents. We weren't wealthy, but we were comfortable. Yet, we occasionally dealt with utility shutoff notices. When I began living independently, I repeated the behaviors I'd observed growing up. I would splurge on frivolous items without thinking about my responsibilities.

When I decided to marry, I hadn't considered my poor financial habits, but that was where I was moving and where I would lead my family. I am much better today because I changed directions and looked "forward."

Then, there's the definition that discusses

"a successful conclusion." This implies that we need to think not just about our marriage's present state but also about its future. My family has been blessed with longevity—my grandfather lived to be ninety-eight and was self-sufficient until the end. But did he, when deciding to marry, consider what the end of that commitment would look like?

What were his thoughts when he moved from the "holler" in West Virginia to the "big city" of Columbus, Ohio? Did he ever envision that his sons would fight for the country? Could he have imagined that he would see over one hundred direct descendants across four generations from his marriage to one woman?

All these things are verifiably true. But would any of this align with what my grandfather considered the result of a successful marriage?

This leads us to the following definition, which incorporates the phrase "toward the future." This concept differs from the previous one because the future is unending. This is particularly challenging for couples, especially since we often focus on the past. A blend of beliefs, values, and experiences shapes our perspective. What we were taught as children, life experiences, and core values all contribute to who we are and who we will become.

Each day offers new experiences and perspectives that shape us. As we glean lessons from our past, we continue to evolve. Our identity is constantly emerging, even when we resist change or new experiences.

The key to benefiting from our experiences lies in the word "willingness"—a willingness to live in the moment. In a Psychology Today article entitled "The Art of Now: Six Steps to Living in the Moment" by Jay Dixit (Psychology Today Article), we find steps that I firmly believe will strengthen and enhance our marriages:

- **To improve your performance, stop thinking about it (unselfconsciousness).** We must stop overthinking. Constant rumination on past actions or future possibilities only brings anxiety and decreases our efficacy. Living in the moment requires setting aside self-consciousness. We need to focus on the present and be aware of our surroundings. Doing so will help reduce anxiety and allow us to savor the moment.

- **To avoid worrying about the future, focus on the present (savoring).** Dixit writes, "Often, we're so trapped in thoughts of the future or the past that we forget to experience—let alone enjoy—what's happening right now." We compare our current situation with the past, failing to appreciate the present. The quality of today's coffee doesn't need to compete with last week's; it should be enjoyed for what it is.
- **If you want a future with your significant other, inhabit the present (breathe).** Being mindful of the moment means we must

"inhabit the present." Deep breathing allows us to realize our current state and take control of the moment, rather than being controlled by it. This deep, relaxing breath serves as a psychological "chill pill," enabling us to truly inhabit the moment.

- **To make the most of your time, lose track of it (flow).** When I lived in Miami Beach, Florida, tourists were easy to spot because they were always rushing. With limited time, they tried to cram in as much as possible, missing the relaxation that the pace of life in Miami offers.

When you stop looking at your watch and get into the flow, your entire outlook changes. Trying to see everything Miami offers robs you of enjoying what you do see. You have to relax and go with the flow. Let yourself be filled with each moment and let the flow carry you on to the next.

Making the most of each moment allows us to experience the next fully.

- **If something bothers you, move toward rather than away from it (acceptance).** The fight-or-flight response isn't the answer to life's irritations.

The more we focus on or internalize our problems, the greater they become and the less likely we are to resolve them. The battle automatically sways in favor of the problem.

Acceptance says, "Thanks, problem, for coming. I have a guesthouse prepared for you. You can visit for a short while, but you can't stay."

Embrace your problem and allow it to flow through you. Ignore a problem, and it will move from the guesthouse and take up residence in your life.

- **Know that you don't know (engagement).** Sometimes, my wife says that we discussed something and that I agreed or said this or that. The problem is that I have no recollection of the discussion and, indeed, not what I said. Unfortunately, that is because I may have been there for the conversation, but I was not in the conversation. My mind was nowhere near the moment. I had checked out. The term "engagement" is about being in the moment.

Our thoughts may sometimes wander, but we must consciously rein them back in. Stay focused on anything new or different about those with you and what they are doing or saying. Choose to appreciate and be empathetic with others and their interests. This will be your special tool to keep you in the moment and allow you to stay engaged.

We may miss each day's blessing and value when we cannot stay focused.

"Let the morning bring me

> word of your unfailing love, for I have put my trust in you. Show me the way I should go, for to you, I entrust my life."
>
> — PSALM 143:8 NIV

> "It is because of the Lord's loving kindnesses that we are not consumed, because His [tender] compassions never fail. They are new every morning; great and beyond measure is Your faithfulness."
>
> — LAMENTATIONS 3:22-23 AMP

One way of moving beyond yesterday and the grip of the past is to commit to keeping our focus on the promising expression "from this day forward." We begin focusing our thoughts on God and His love for us every day.

That kind of personal posture of being mindful of how He moves on our behalf will birth within us the flow of His love and care that will frame our responses and our entire relationship with our spouse.

❧ 4 ☙
FOR BETTER, FOR WORSE

Let's focus on the message of Ephesians 5:22-33 from The Message Bible for a moment.

> *Wives, understand and support your husbands in ways that show your support for Christ. The husband provides leadership to his wife the way Christ does to his church, not by domineering but by cherishing. So just as the church submits to Christ as he exercises such leadership, wives*

should likewise submit to their husbands.

Husbands, go all out in your love for your wives, exactly as Christ did for the church—a love marked by giving, not getting. Christ's love makes the church whole. His words evoke her beauty. Everything he does and says is designed to bring the best out of her, dressing her in dazzling white silk, radiant with holiness. And that is how husbands ought to love their wives. They're really doing themselves a favor—since they're already "one" in marriage.

No one abuses his own body, does he? No, he feeds and pampers it. That's how Christ treats us, the church, since we are part of his body. And this is why a man leaves father and mother and cherishes his wife. No longer

ESTABLISHING GLORY 3

two, they become "one flesh." This is a huge mystery, and I don't pretend to understand it all. What is clearest to me is the way Christ treats the church. And this provides a good picture of how each husband is to treat his wife, loving himself in loving her, and how each wife is to honor her husband.

These verses are some of the most misconstrued words in scripture.

So, while I will not start being "preachy," I want us to take time to look at the background of what the Apostle Paul is saying.

Did you notice words like support, leadership, cherishing, giving, beauty, and, of course, love to describe the nature of our relationship as husband and wife? The tone of this passage is that we are not to "lord it over" one another, but to serve each other. Selflessness is the very essence of loving another.

Often people want to point to the phrase about women "submitting to their husbands" and start shouting "chauvinism!" But nothing could be further from the truth. This is about selflessness, focusing on the husband to serve at his side with the purpose of moving him forward toward the responsibilities that rest on him.

Those responsibilities, if you read on, are focused on treating his wife with the selflessness modeled after Christ, who gave Himself lovingly for His bride, the Church.

We are admonished to focus on each other and selflessly be the conduit of grace and strength that allows the other to grow more and more into the person God wants them to be. We are to live in mutual submission to the needs and well-being of the other, just as Christ does for each of us.

These verses, however, do not specifically raise the question of "when." When are we supposed to do all this loving, cherishing, and supporting? When are we to submit to each other? When it's convenient and these things all line up like the stars? When it's inconvenient, are we still supposed to do all of that?

If we get honest about marriage, we know it isn't all cotton candy and unicorns. Life is hard enough by itself, but when you combine two lives, things can get quite perplexing, complicated, and even scary.

But the answer to "when" is in the model of Jesus. There is no specific "when." There is only the constant and unlimited, always present and in place selflessness that showers us with the kind of love we are to have with each other.

JACKIE SMITH, JR.

FOR BETTER

My first business, Anointed Ministries, was a computer company that sold and repaired computers, provided website design and consultation, and offered training for everyone from the novice to the advanced user. It was great!

I was a one-man band. I designed and printed my business cards, and everywhere I went, I would leave a card, hoping that someone would pick it up and use our services. Then, one day, someone did.

I had gone to the doctor for an outpatient procedure and gave one of my cards to the attending physician. His unexpected response was an invitation to lunch.

I told my wife about the doctor wanting to have lunch, and we were both uber-excited! This was finally happening! We were going to finally get a customer!

You see, I started Anointed Ministries because I was laid off. I was the "Corporate Training Manager," and we had just expanded training from an individual location to multiple locations in several states. We had initiated everything from one-on-one coaching to packed classrooms. We were growing and becoming profitable.

Then, I landed my first big contract for over $100,000. Life was indeed "For Better."

During this time, I received a raise, and we were finally getting caught up on all our bills. I started paying my tithes faithfully and even started doing more volunteering at our church.

Then, one day, the owner called a meeting with the entire organization. We had to make some changes, and unfortunately, we had to make some staff changes.

It was a very somber moment for everyone, but while I felt terrible for those who would lose their jobs, I was confident I wouldn't be. My department was growing like wildfire.

Well, take a wild guess who the first person who was called into the office was.

The company was changing direction and had decided that the training program was no longer needed. So, "thank you for your hard work and dedication. Your services are no longer required."

I was devastated.

Our life just went from better to worse in one moment. How do I tell my wife? How are we going to get our bills paid? How will we survive?

Then, came the "God questions:" How could He let this happen to us? Why did God leave us hanging? I'm paying tithes and volunteering, and this is how God responds?

We get a little sanctimonious at times, don't we? We blame God for our troubles and forget that He loves us more than we will ever know. And He has a plan for our lives.

Act 2, stage right: Enter my brand-new company and this lunch with my doctor.

I'm dressed for the occasion in business casual attire. We met at a nice restaurant and had a conversation about my new venture. He loved it, but he felt there was a problem. It wasn't the services and my sales abilities; it was my company name, "Anointed Ministries."

He said, "It sounds like 'Have Bible, Will Travel' and makes no reference to all of this computer work that you do. You have to change your name to get the business that you're looking for."

I took his words to heart, closed Anointed Ministries, and started over with "AM Computer Services, Inc." (As you may have guessed, "AM" stood for "Anointed Ministries," but I never told anyone that.)

MAKING A CHANGE

Making this change meant that my marriage had to endure more money spent on a dream while I was collecting unemployment. Right before the layoff, we had caught up on our mortgage, and now we were in arrears again. We had a humble life, and things were super tight. We had those typical arguments about time, money, and everything else.

"For worse" was happening to us.

When things truly got bad, I started thinking about quitting this fantasy of being my own boss and getting a regular job with a steady income and maybe benefits to help my marriage. Even I thought I would "fall on the sword," take one for the team, and hopefully, one day, I would try again.

"For worse" was getting even worse.

I tell this story because many, if not most, marriages fail because of financial issues. Today, most of us are only one or two paychecks away from poverty. Having a savings plan or emergency money only covers a bill or two for at best a few weeks.

What happens when we go through such circumstances? What happens when we run out of unemployment benefits? What are we supposed to do when "For worse" isn't just knocking on the door but has moved in and is in the kitchen making sandwiches or sitting on your bed watching TV?

Husbands, we may be aware of and even struggle with our responsibility to be the protectors of our homes, but we may easily miss the fact that our wives are struggling with us. Not only are things happening to us as a family, but these things affect each of us in very personal ways. We have to be understanding enough to acknowledge the pain that our wives and children are going through.

The most significant attribute needed by everyone in the family is understanding. During times of hardship, each spouse is to be mutually concerned about each other's stress. Together, they must find solutions to cope, share the search for answers, and avoid the remarks that sound uncaring or even like nagging. To keep harping on bills that need to be paid or that little Johnny still needs braces only wears each other down.

Support is a partnership.

When we take on the roles of husband and wife, we step into a partnership agreement that says, "I've got your back, no matter what." That's easy when we live in "For Better." But the real challenge comes with "For worse."

When we married each other, we truly became partners in life, and that life partnership extends into every aspect of living, and there's nothing we can't overcome together.

JACKIE SMITH, JR.

Shortly after changing my business's name, we landed our first contract, and things turned around for my business, my marriage, and my life, not just because of the money but because of the commitment my wife and I have for each other in every aspect of our life together.

5
FOR RICHER, FOR POORER: BEYOND MONEY

When 99% of us think about the phrase "for richer, for poorer," we usually focus on money and financial well-being. But, as with everything else, there are more layers than we often see.

When defined, "rich" refers not only to "having a great deal of money or assets; wealthy" but also has these other definitions:

- Plentiful; abundant.
- Producing a large quantity of something.

- Interesting because full of diversity or complexity.

Along with having wealth in the form of money and assets, we need to have a mixture of the other riches as well.

What does it mean to have a plentiful and abundant marriage?

Think of a Red Velvet cake with its unique texture, bold color, exquisite icing, and flavor. Now, picture a large piece of that cake sitting in front of you. Your eyes are fixated on the plate, your nose is filling with the aroma, and you can barely control the growing anticipation of that first taste.

And then it happens. You bring that waiting fork to your mouth. The flavor is so rich you can barely stand it. Your taste buds are nearly overwhelmed. And you vow nothing will stop you from devouring the entire piece.

Marriages should be every bit as pleasantly overwhelming. Life together is to overflow with richness that you vow you never want to be without.

I have been living that experience, so I

want to share with you one way the aroma of love is evidenced in our family.

I was born in August. So, (hold on to your seats) I celebrate my birth for the entire month!

When I first told my wife about my birth-month celebrations, she didn't believe me. I tried to warn her, but some things you need to experience for yourself. Of course, I wanted to know how she wanted to celebrate her birthday in June.

Her reply: "We can just do dinner with some family and friends."

My reply: "Is that it?"

So, when June rolled around, I did as she requested, and we had a lovely party for her. She enjoyed herself, and her celebration ended the day after her party.

Then came July 31!

We went out to eat, and I proclaimed, "Happy Birth Month, Day Zero!"

Her reaction (classic, but with a puzzled expression): "Day Zero? Your birthday month doesn't start until tomorrow!"

My response (with a twinkle in my eye): "Have you ever heard of Christmas Eve?"

And so began the celebration.

We celebrated every single day of the month! We attended outdoor concerts, went to my favorite restaurants, cooked my favorite meals, and the fun was overwhelmingly exhausting!

But the real fun for me was finding something new to do each day. After the 10th day, it started to become a challenge. What could we do today that we haven't already done? How can today be as exciting or more interesting than any of the other days? How can we keep this thing going?

The trick is that, as a team, we had to make this celebration a priority every day. We had to make it unique. And not making an attempt was not an option!

Celebrating Life Together

It was hard working these celebratory events into our daily lives for an entire month! We still went to work every day, the children started back to school, and we didn't miss church. So, my Birth Month celebrations take a toll on us, but it's worth it.

Now, just in case you're thinking I am a self-serving jerk, I'll let you in on a little secret. The real fun for me is giving my family a special time once a year to enjoy something extraordinary together. Sharing this unusual idea with them will not only be memorable for each of us, but we bond together as a family in a unique way.

Our marriages should be like my Happy Birth Month celebrations. Filled with intentional moments as a couple and a family. All of us share the experience of setting aside the routines of life and simply being in the moment.

And of course, I post the shenanigans during this month-long celebration on social media. My friends good-naturedly razz me every year, but hopefully, we will inspire others to celebrate themselves more creatively!

One time, one of my cousins wanted to join us on our excursions. When we live bountifully, people want to be a part of that.

That is a good thing. If no one wants to hang out with us as a couple, then we might want to ask, "Why not?" What are we not doing?

People are naturally drawn to people and things that excite them, motivate them, and cheer them on. So, if my marriage isn't doing that, then we're living in a bubble, or we're doing something wrong.

We are social beings, and we are made to enjoy life together with those around us, and as a couple, we should inspire others with our examples of joy.

Before my wife and I were married, she used to talk about spending time with married couples, going places and enjoying those relationships. I confess, I found that odd. I had not experienced that. Of course, she had been divorced for 20 years.

On the other hand, I had only been recently divorced after being married for 20 years, and married couples didn't spend time with someone who was divorced.

After people get married and return from their honeymoon, they live their lives within their own space. The non-married friends get pushed to the side. Some activities that they did when they were single are now shelved, pushed off into the corner of life because they are too busy keeping up with the new routine of their new family life, focusing on having a well-balanced married life. There is a natural tendency to shift their social life to other married couples.

Oddly enough, the first argument my wife and I had was about not spending enough time together. It was a rather heated exchange and is memorable because she paused mid-stream and said, "Oh my God, we're arguing! Okay, your turn!"

Now, this was more frustrating than the argument itself. And being the stubborn guy that I am, I refused to say anything else. Later we laughed about it, but the underlying concern was never addressed.

But her twist in the moment turned down the temperature on what could have turned into a tempest.

Without proper balance in our social life, married life can usher in, as the chapter title notes, one of the "for poorer" times in our lives. Let's take a second look at this term "poorer."

Again, when we think of richer and poorer, our thoughts are toward finances. But when we look at the non-money definitions of poor, we can see deeper into our lives:

- Worse than is usual, expected, or desirable; of a low or inferior standard or quality.
- (of a person) considered to be deserving of pity or sympathy.

Balancing Life in Marriage

Those definitions remind us that balancing life as a married couple needs to focus on more than just our finances. While it is true that when we get married, life begins anew for us, but the lives we were living separately now require a genuine blending of our expectations, including such things as our social life and our together time. Without coming together in our perspectives about our future, our finances, our social life, many issues we will encounter together, we will find ourselves poorer rather than richer.

This is a particular risk when people marry before they have had time to really mature. Today, young people live in an extended state of adolescence. Many people in their 20s still have outlooks on life that extend their teen years, focused on having fun and unfocused on responsibility.

And when they marry before they have left an adolescent mindset behind, they lack the skills to shift from being self-focused to living centered on someone else. All too often, they drink the Disney juice of 'Happily Ever After' just to find out (borrowing words from Spike Lee's film, "Malcolm X"), that "You've been had! Ya been took! Ya been hoodwinked! Bamboozled! Led astray! Run amok!" And sadly, because they are too immature, it's probably all too true.

They go to bed one night with the love of their life, the perfect mate that they have "laid down their life for," and they wake up the next morning with the dread of another day when their spouse irritates the life out of them and with a nagging question about why they married him or her.

The idea of a prosperous and happy marriage has faded, and the fog of "poor" has settled in. Where is the love? What happened?

Most times, the problem is that the "love" they have had to this point has been mostly made up of emotion. They have placed so much weight on feeling, and when the feelings are replaced by a less glamorous part of being together, their motivation to blend and bond has begun to drown in the pool of "poor."

Love is not just something we are to feel, but something we must commit to do.

To be fair, many marriages, even for those who are supposed to be mature, fail because one or both stops doing love. To feel love, you have to do love! When the doing disappears, the feelings do as well, and then we start down the path of separation, divorce, and dissolution.

So, what does 'doing love' look like?

ESTABLISHING GLORY 3

1 Corinthians 13 MSG describes love this way:

- Love never gives up.
- Love cares more for others than for self.
- Love doesn't want what it doesn't have.
- Love doesn't strut,
- Doesn't have a swelled head,
- Doesn't force itself on others,
- Isn't always "me first,"
- Doesn't fly off the handle,
- Doesn't keep score of the sins of others,
- Doesn't revel when others grovel,
- Takes pleasure in the flowering of truth,
- Puts up with anything,
- Trusts God always,
- Always looks for the best,
- Never looks back,
- But keeps going to the end.
- Love never dies.

Doing Love: The Key to a Rich Marriage

That's what doing love looks like. When we stop doing any of those things, we are no longer experiencing the riches of genuine love. If any of those "tasks of love" are missing, then love is being forfeited. This is not a list of options, but a single formula. If one element is missing, this love formula is rendered impotent.

When you give up on the person who you love, you've given up love for that person. We must be vigilant, or we'll lose both! A love-filled marriage requires work!

If my spouse is keeping a running tab of how often I've failed her, how many times I didn't keep my word or upset her, then the rest of the list is meaningless. No matter what I do for her, however good it may be, she's still keeping that other list.

If I'm always getting upset about what my spouse is saying or doing, am I helping or hurting our love connection? My self-focus that feeds my rage is obviously not loving toward her, and the rest of that formula no longer enriches her. They are of no value.

That, my friend, is the work we need to do, the effort we need to put into our marriages.

"Poorer" is a state of being, a mindset, or a spirit. We are by nature "poor" because putting someone else ahead of us is unnatural. But there is a rich, new nature that replaces our self-focus with a genuine love that values someone else as more important than yourself.

If we are to overcome the poverty of a marriage and successfully experience a rich relationship, we have to acknowledge the natural self-centeredness that makes our relationship poorer. And no matter who you are, you will have to face and deal with your own personal poverty that lives so naturally in you.

I once saw an article from Focus on the Family by Mitch Temple called "Ten Secrets to a Successful Marriage"[1]. Here is the list of "secrets":

1. Happiness is not the most important thing.
2. Couples discover the value in just showing up.
3. If you do what you always do, you will get the same result.
4. Your attitude does matter.
5. Change your mind, change your marriage.
6. The grass is greenest where you water it.
7. You can change your marriage by changing yourself.
8. Love is a verb, not just a feeling.
9. Marriage is often about fighting the battle between your ears.
10. A crisis doesn't mean the marriage is over.

The author has a lot to say about each point, but the most important take-away is that to shift from poorer to richer, you have to realize that it is not about the other person. It's about me. It's about you. We must take responsibility for our love, our marriage, our relationship, and fight for them, whether we're in times of plenty or leanness.

It's up to me, it's up to you!

6
IN SICKNESS AND IN HEALTH: A REFLECTION ON MARRIAGE VOWS

Unlike the other parts of the wedding vows, this chapter is straightforward. There are just a couple of definitions of sickness:

- The state of being ill.
- The feeling or fact of being affected with nausea or vomiting.

Health, on the other hand, is defined as:

- The state of being free from illness or injury.

- A person's mental or physical condition.

The fact that the marriage vows include sickness and health says that sickness and health can influence whether or not a couple stays together.

But why? When you have chosen to be with this special person "from this day forward," doesn't that automatically include their well-being? Or yours?

Health and beauty are two of the most promoted yet elusive topics in our society.

When I was 22, I had just got out of the United States Air Force. I was the picture of health; a tall, sexy, chocolate, 6-foot-3-inch dreamboat (or so I was told), with 20/20 vision, a well-defined six-pack, and I weighed in at a smooth 130. I had a full head of hair (emphasis on had). I was as "healthy as a horse!" There was nothing that hindered me from doing what I wanted and being who I wanted to be. Life was grand!

That was then, and this is now (26 years later). I shrunk an inch. I not only wear glasses, but I have bifocals. That six-pack now looks like I'm 6 months pregnant. And at 230 lbs., I've gained a whole 'nother me!

And about that full head of hair, those beautiful locks have receded so far back that I have a lot in common with a cue ball. And if I were to compare myself to a horse now, they would put me out to pasture with my collection of medications for allergies, vitamin D deficiency, acid reflux, high cholesterol, and let's not forget, diabetes.

How many times have we chosen a mate primarily based on looks, physical features, or the activities that they're involved in? The problem is that as time progresses, our ideas change, so much so that excellent health and matchless beauty are put at the bottom of the list if not removed altogether.

Do you remember when the socially ideal woman was the envied figure 8, 36-24-36? All the parts seemed to fit just right, and the ladies would work to get to this size or close to it. Then, several years later, the bar for "perfection" no longer mentioned measurements. The focus was on sizes, and the perfect size was zero! And if you went by all the popular magazines, any lady who was not a zero was not considered as beautiful. So, the great push was just to decrease dress sizes. Now, there has been another shift. Big wasn't just accepted; it has replaced the old ideal of zero. We started seeing full-figured manikins in stores, and shows like "My 600-lb Life" are mainstream phenomena!

This is a peculiar time because all three shifts are now being displayed and considered as equally acceptable and applauded in today's society. There has been less of a change in what is seen regarding men, but inclusiveness seems less pressing for them.

There are many people who are not satisfied with their health or beauty. So, they buy not only gym memberships, weight-loss programs, and pay for bariatric surgeries, options that are all now common everyday trends.

Balancing Health and Commitment in Marriage

But how does all this play into our marriages? This unreasonable lack of balance in how we think about what is healthy or not can quickly turn what could have been a prosperous and healthy relationship into a poor and unhealthy one.

I know a husband who told his wife she was getting fat; if she didn't fix it, he was leaving. The reason for her weight gain was the medication she took to save her life, but that didn't seem to factor into this man's thinking. And she had only gained ten pounds. Threats of divorce for gaining 10 pounds? Really?

By no means am I advocating obesity or being overweight. I am saying, however, that each of us needs to care for ourselves and exercise healthy self-love. We don't need to compare ourselves to anyone else, but we should take the steps required to be our best.

But we need to focus on other kinds of health, specifically mental and spiritual health.

Let's be honest. Marriage is an institution, and some people jokingly talk about mental health and marriage in the same breath as a kind of oxymoron (something like seriously funny, acting naturally, or deafening silence).

Others might light-heartedly compare the institution of marriage with another institution, specifically an insane asylum.

The interesting thing is that as a married couple, you'll experience *all* those oxymorons within your marriage! After all, the idea of commitment comes up in both cases.

But all joking aside, the institution of marriage involves a commitment that does not fluctuate.

My ex-wife was diagnosed with mental challenges, including depression, multiple personalities, and bipolar disorder. And I loved her very much.

We had our usual marital troubles, like any other couple. But there were those other moments, those times when I watched her change into another person and try to hurt her own teenage child.

Love requires real grit. Sometimes, you have to make tough decisions. You have to love someone enough to do what will make them safe or to ensure that they get the proper help to cope and get well. Other times, you may have to acknowledge that you cannot help. In my case, my ex and I moved forward separately. We didn't give up on each other, but we gave up on the marriage.

While this book is about fixing and keeping marriages together, there are moments when we realize the situation is beyond your ability to change it. When that happens, you may have to face another side of marriage: how to bring it to an end. I'm not advocating that choice, but as hard as you may want to fix the relationship, both have to be able and willing to work at it.

There are clearly some specific challenges that we cannot change. We can get counseling before we are married, but sometimes, all the good intentions in the world are not enough to fix what is wrong.

Let me assure you that pre-marital counseling is one of the most important steps you can take. Couples considering marriage have eyes clouded with amorous expectations and broad (often somewhat unrealistic) dreams. Counseling helps them look at their plans realistically and consider their decisions and what they involve. The process is not designed to let them stare only at their delightful dreams. Instead, a counselor can help them prepare for some of the unavoidable unpleasantness they will experience.

One of the most significant benefits of pre-marital counseling is the potential to discover who they are and how to be transparent with each other in their relationship, even during their courtship.

All too often, we get married to the person who we each have *represented* ourselves to be rather than who they *really* are.

During the courting stage, we should start peeling back those layers of persona and be honest with that potential candidate. For example, I was a horrible money manager. So, I covered my poor money skills with payday loans and credit cards. But that persona has a short lifespan because eventually, the commitment of marriage will unmask the pretension.

Soon after getting married, the frustration of my mounting bills affected our relationship.

We had to decide to address these issues together. Otherwise, my poor financial skills would have bankrupted both of us.

In short, I may have been able to avoid most of the drama in my first two marriages if we would have gone through pre-marital counseling.

So now, what about our spiritual health?

In 2 Corinthians 6:14 KJV, we read, *"Be ye not unequally yoked together with unbelievers: for what fellowship hath righteousness with unrighteousness? and what communion hath light with darkness?"*

The condensed version: our core beliefs should match or be compatible. As with anything else, there are ample examples of couples whose fundamental beliefs don't match up. There are exceptions, but that is not the rule. I have several friends whose central values are vastly different. For example, one husband is Muslim, and the wife is Catholic. They have a fantastic family and are great friends. But again, they are the exception. We'll talk more about this in Chapter 9.

The question is, how are we to deal with the spectrum of health challenges?

Whether we are dealing with physical, mental, or spiritual illness, our response should always be the same. We are to be conduits of grace and healing. Giving up on our spouse in their times of need is not an option.

My parents are a vivid example of this commitment to their vows.

They lived average lives, raised their children into adulthood, and supported other families within the community by "adopting" children from all over the neighborhood. Every time I turned around, someone else was called son or daughter, and my parents loved and cared for each one.

And then came the stunning interruption of breast cancer in the pleasantness of our lives. My mom was stricken with a very rare form of breast cancer. It was found in only one of her breasts, but it affected the lives of our entire family. We all watched as my dad never left her side. He was at every appointment and active in the decisions that were made. He was a soldier! My mom, being full of faith, told the doctors that God was going to heal her and that they would be amazed by the hand of God in her life. So, she never went through any chemotherapy or radiation. The miracle is that she went in for a follow-up visit, and the doctors couldn't find the cancerous cells. Yes, God had healed her! And my dad was right there at every turn!

Then we faced a new fight with the dread of breast cancer!

This time, the cancer attacked my mom's other breast, and it was an altogether different type of breast cancer, again, very rare. This time, my mom went through chemotherapy and radiation. And again, my dad was right there, at every turn, faithfully supporting his wife.

My mom was given the all-clear from the new battle with cancer! Her hands were raised in victory, like the hands of the champion boxer at the end of the match! She was evidence that when God wins a battle, He wins completely! There is no such thing as a partial victory with God. So, this new battle with cancer was met with a new victory. And my dad was right there! But then came the diagnosis of lung cancer, the final fight!

To use the boxing analogy, my mom was Muhammad Ali. Cancer #1 was Sonny Liston, defeated in a major upset. Cancer #2 was "The Rumble in the Jungle" against George Foreman, again defeated by a knockout. Notice that each fight had a different opponent, but the results were still the same. Ali won! My mom won! And my dad was right there in her corner, rooting her on to victory!

My mom's lung cancer was like Ali's Parkinson's disease. It was still a battle, but this fight took her out of the ring - always a champion but no longer fighting. On July 14, 2000, God decided that her battle was over and retired her gloves. And, in championship form, my dad was right there!

I pray often that God would allow me to catch the mantle of my father. If I can have even a portion of this man's faith, a measure of his virtue and faithfulness that he displayed as he journeyed with Mom through those battles and valleys, I will be the husband that

I need to be. His example showed that genuine love gives no license to walk away in the face of illness.

When taking the marriage vows, we must recognize the commitment that we are making, vows that truly hold fast in every situation. Faithfulness to those vows is easy when everything works well and everyone is healthy. But there will be moments when we may have to care for our spouse during battles with any number of illnesses. Will you accept the challenge as a champion or wave a white flag and wimp out?

7
TO LOVE AND TO CHERISH

Cynthia Hand, the author of "Boundless," says, "Love is a many-splendored thing. But it is also a pain in the a." I wholeheartedly agree with the first half of her statement, and I know there can be some truth to the second sometimes. Love is many things, but to avoid what she calls the pain of it, we need to truly understand the many flavors of love and how they work in our lives.

Have you heard the expression "searching for our soulmate"? Well, this is the epitome of erroneous thinking. Soulmates aren't found.

You don't just meet someone, have a 10-minute conversation with them, and suddenly, they're your soulmate.

The Urban Dictionary defines a soulmate like this:

> "It's like a best friend, but more. It's the one person in the world that knows you better than anyone else. It's someone who makes you a better person, well, actually they don't make you a better person, you do that yourself because they inspire you. A soulmate is someone who you carry with you forever. It's the one person who knew you, and accepted you, and believed in you before anyone else did or when no one else would. And no matter what happens... you'll always love them."

Does any of that sound like some random person who you met on the street?

Here's a profound truth: Soul mates are not "found," they are created!

Unfortunately, we place so much stock in ideologies that we miss the truth. Truth says that when we open our hearts to people, we are giving them access to something extraordinary. How they treat that access builds or destroys any future relationship with that person or with anyone else.

Let's talk about John and Jane.

While John was going through the divorce process, he met Jane. There was mutual interest between them, and they pursued a relationship.

In full disclosure, John told Jane that he was going through a divorce and gave her the details of what was going on. Unfortunately, Jane didn't believe him.

She had been down this road before with married men (technically; you are married until the divorce decree has been finalized). Other guys had told her they were divorced or getting divorced. They established relationships with her. They dated for extended amounts of time, then one day she finds out that there was no divorce, and there was never a conversation of one. In one instance, Jane found out that her guy and his wife never filed for divorce and announced that they were going to have a child!

So, Jane was more than a little distrustful of John.

This story is relevant because John didn't allow her experiences to deter him from pursuing and eventually marrying Jane. He didn't let up and continued being friends with her. He didn't force himself on her.

He loved her, and his love guided them. He knew she was the desire of his heart.

By no means was this an easy venture. They went through lots of successes and failures. They "broke-up" several times, went over a month without seeing each other, and even saw other people. But when it came down to it, he loved her and wasn't going to allow her to get away.

During those months, they became soulmates. They connected at a deeper level because of everything that they had gone through together. They've been married for a while now. They have their challenges, but through their shared experiences, they grew together: #Soulmates.

This is not to be confused with soulmate's second cousin, Soul Tie.

One of my concerns with today's American society is that, amid John and Jane's story, "they saw other people." Meaning, at some point, John slept with someone other than Jane. And she did the same thing! Neither of them has the "moral high ground" in this instance. Both of them opened up to someone outside of their partnership.

Giving of oneself sexually or even deeply emotionally opens the door to the physical transference of bodily fluids, sweat, saliva, and other juices. It kicks open the door for emotional and spiritual connections beyond the physical act.

When we give ourselves sexually to another, we are exchanging a part of ourselves with them. Again, this is an exchange. They are giving us a part of them as well.

According to a report from HealthLine, Inc., entitled "What's the Average Person's Number of Sexual Partners?" (see link), residents in Louisiana (where the study originated) were found to average 15.7 sexual partners! There is a lot of "exchanging" going on! But how does that affect us overall?

"Soul ties" are powerful because the connection doesn't just go away. The soul tie can linger for years when a spouse is lost through death or divorce. If you remarry, it is not uncommon for the name of the former spouse to show up unexpectedly when introducing the new spouse to a friend or appear instinctively at a significantly emotional moment. And if the connection or "tie" results from a less structured relationship, the result can be just as instinctive. You may have been upset at something your significant other has said or done, and instinctively, the name of another partner is heard coming out of your mouth!

The apologies and the back-pedaling start immediately, but the soul tie has impacted the moment.

The imprint of a soul tie may be experienced internally as well. Mary walks by, and she's wearing a particular perfume that so-and-so used to wear, and for the rest of the day, you can't get so-and-so off your mind. You start down memory lane and must resist the urge to pick up the phone. That's a "soul tie" diversion.

But the bond of a soul tie can be broken. If you have experienced a soul tie because of an illicit relationship, Sheila Wray Gregoire, author of the article "To Love, Honor, & Vacuum; Soul Ties: How to Break Them and Live in Freedom,"[1] provides clear steps to be free of that bond.

1. Accept Forgiveness
2. Confess
3. Fill your mind with goodness
4. Purge Fantasies
5. Pray and move forward in victory!

To move the discussion on into loving and cherishing, any soul ties need to be broken and discarded.

JACKIE SMITH, JR.

LOVE

According to an article in Psychology Today[2], these are the seven types of love:

1. Eros is sexual or passionate love, the type most akin to our modern construct of romantic love.
2. The hallmark of Philia, or friendship, is shared goodwill.
3. Storge ('store-gae'), or familial love, is a kind of Philia pertaining to the love between parents and their children.
4. Agape is universal love, such as the love for strangers, nature, or God.
5. Ludus is playful or uncommitted love.
6. Pragma is a kind of practical love founded on reason or duty and one's longer-term interests.
7. Philautia is self-love, which can be healthy or unhealthy.

Scholars consider Agape to be the highest

form of love. While its meaning is centered loosely on "charity," it primarily refers to God's love, the same love that He wants us to experience and express. Some suggest that a child's innocent nature and trust instinct are an expression of agape, which may be true in some measure. But the child also has received from his spiritual heritage the fallen nature that soon is evidenced as he grows and meaningfully functions in a fallen world.

Agape is God's gift to lift us above the lesser perceptions of love. But in our focus on marriage, we cannot deny that, prior to marriage, most relationships display a mix of playfulness without sincere concern for commitment (Philia, mixed with Ludus). Some will shift from the many casual relationships to the eros kind of love. The passion of eros is most often sexual. Unfortunately, our current culture has so idolized sexuality that many people define this lesser form of love as the most desirable and become stuck at that level.

When we get married, while the sexuality (eros) that God created us with is undeniably part of this relationship, a maturing marriage increasingly shifts to a more familial texture. The spiritual bond of marriage calls us to raise the bar from eros and the self-focus of philautia to an ever-maturing expression of agape. The "I" is increasingly replaced with "us," and with agape, our relationships are reflections of His plan for our bond of love.

The kids come along and the familial storge expression of love now blends with agape.

To be true lovers, we must learn the art of balancing each of these forms, always blending them with the love God has enabled us to share.

I was once asked, "Do you love your ex?"

My answer was and is a resounding, "Yes."

That may seem unnatural, but let's look a little deeper. When I married, love was one vow and the sum total of the vows. And when I was divorced, my commitment to love could not be set aside. The responsibility doesn't go away. But the love changes because the nature of the relationship changes.

Understandably, I no longer have an eros

connection with her. I haven't seen or spoken to one of my exes in over 30 years, but the agape love that God has enabled me to experience is extended to everyone, and that includes my exes. The love is not reflective of our former relationship but reflects how God cares and sees them. So, I am to let His agape love be extended to everyone.

Think about that for a moment. The human reaction to a broken relationship is often less than amicable. Too many times, it is far less than kind. But agape love is to be our guide, and there is no room for hate or fear.

Remember Cynthia Hand's definition of love at the beginning of this chapter: "Love is a many-splendored thing. But it is also a pain in the a**."

To avoid love from being a pain in the rear, we have to level the playing field continually. All the times we have irritated, disappointed, or even hurt each other must be put away, put out of sight. We must start a new scorecard and reset our love to zero often. We all need a clean slate and a fresh start. I know that this flies in the face of our claim to "love each other more every day," but when we start keeping score and measuring our love by performance levels, we should ask ourselves if what we have is truly love. If we keep a ledger with negatives compared to positives, our focus is no longer on our spouse but on ourselves and what we are getting or missing in the relationship. Keeping a tally is not part of genuine love.

My wife loves me, but I am not always easy to love. I get cranky, too busy or distracted. I have times when I have not been very understanding or even too self-centered. She doesn't love me because I am a perfect husband. Some looking on might even say that I am unlovable. But she never stops loving me.

And from time to time, the roles may be reversed, but I never stop loving her.

We love each other even in challenging times, even when we are not at our best.

But we are not keeping score. Our choice to love when the other is going through unpleasantness and may be "out of sorts" doesn't make us winners. If there is a winner, then there must be a loser.

Keeping score can lead to the habit of pettiness. One of us fixed our plate before the other one. She didn't say "I love you" the last time she left the house. I didn't open the car door for her.

So, does that make either of us less loving? Are we winners and losers?

No!

We both need to hit the reset button, throw away the tired ledgers, and shift our outlook so we can experience the agape-filled relationship that looks beyond each other's weak moments and see each other through God's eyes.

Recently, I had an attack of pettiness. I was looking at my wife's Facebook account and realized that almost all the activity came from me or her friends tagging her in our posts. Then, I looked at her Instagram page and was like, "I don't see any pictures of me!" But when people see my Facebook and Instagram pages, she's all over them!

I realized I had an attitude toward her social media accounts. Why wasn't she posting pictures of me? Do people know that she's married? And I wondered who was sending her messages because her husband wasn't on display.

The more I thought about it, the more bothered I got until I started putting things into perspective. My wife isn't a social media poster. She's a 'stalker.' She is the one who visits other people's pages and sees what they are doing, whereas I am a poster and hardly ever look at other people's pages.

So, am I a better spouse because I post? Is she less of a spouse because she doesn't?

I had to check myself. Marriage isn't a spousal competition. It's not about who can show the world the most posts about their spouse. We must remember that we all display love differently, and that revelation solidifies our growth. There are no individual winners. We win together!

CHERISH

To cherish is to protect and care for someone or something. It is holding something or someone with a sense of expectation or hope, with anticipation or keeping hope or ambition in our minds. Cherishing our spouse should look like a sweet embrace and affection.

Here's an excerpt from the lyrics by Kool & The Gang, who performed a song called "Cherish":

> *The world is always changing*
> *Nothing stays the same*
> *But love will stand the test of time*
> *The next life that we live in*
> *Remains to be seen*
> *Will you be by my side*
> *I often pray before I lay down by your side*
> *If you receive your calling before I awake*
> *Could I make it through the night*
> *Cherish the love we have*
> *We should cherish the life we live*
> *Cherish the love*
> *Cherish the life*

One thing that happens in marriage is that we get consumed with life's challenges. We wake up just to go to work. We work only to pay bills. We eat dinner, then go to bed, just to repeat the cycle over and over. But when we look back on our lives, where are the high points of our marriages? What special moments did we have? Did we create any of these special moments, or did we just pass the time? Let's be intentional in our love for each other.

When my children were young, we gave up on Halloween and Trick-or-Treat. There had been far too many reports of tampering with the candy, and I was done with it.

The sad part is that my children, like others, still wanted to participate in beggar's night. So, I made a deal with them. Instead of going out, we'd do something special, like a party or something.

They were excited at first.

All was good until they saw the other children outside going door to door. We ended up having dinner, watching one of their favorite shows on TV, then off to bed.

While they were sleeping, my wife and I rode to the store. I got a bag of mixed candies for the children for no particular reason, just "because."

Well, I'm not one to do anything small if I can help it. "A" bag of candy was almost $100 worth of candy!

And I didn't just present the candy to the children. I turned the house into Candyland!

There was candy everywhere! The living room was filled with candy. There was candy covering the pool table. Candy lined the stairs. Their bedroom floors and dressers were layered in candy. We even put candy in their shoes and their beds (while they slept). It was a diabetic nightmare, and it was AWESOME!

We had candy for a YEAR...

When the children woke up and saw all that candy, they put on their Halloween costumes and went crazy!

I genuinely cherish moments like this. It does my heart good to remember all the love moments that we've created in our home.

We have to fight the urge to focus on what's wrong in life. Our lives can be fun and exciting! But again, we have to be intentional about it.

One of the most relaxed moments that my wife and I share is merely lying in bed with my wife's head on my chest. We work so hard that when it's time for bed, we pass out. But holding her in my arms is a fantastic feeling. And from time to time, we remind each other that a cuddle is required.

I cherish those moments. Some moments fill your heart. Are you actively making those moments happen, or are you just waiting for them? Well, don't hold your breath! Life has a way of consuming our energy if we let it!

Make it happen!

8
TILL DEATH DO US PART

As odd as it may sound, we need to begin this chapter like the others, with a definition of our subject. What is this thing called death?

Death...

- The action or fact of dying or being killed; the end of the life of a person or organism.

When I started thinking about 'till death do us part," my mind went directly to the first definition—someone died, and the marriage is over. But the longer I thought about it, the more intrigued I became with this part of the vows.

Most times, we are primarily focused on the fact of death (see definition #1), and except for physical death, we may often glaze over the why (the second and third definitions). That is particularly true when discussing the end of a relationship and even more so when a marriage dies.

But let's start by affirming that marriage represents life. A marriage that has ended (whatever the reason) no longer has life. The soul tie may linger, but the life of the marriage relationship is lost.

The death of a marriage primarily takes place in three ways: physical death, desertion, or divorce. In any of those causes, people will experience sadness, anger, confusion, grief, or the struggle of being alone. Those are all natural responses in dealing with the fact of death or loss. Acknowledging that loss, however, is not the same as understanding it and grappling with why it occurred.

An enlightening report from a Medical Examiner[1] discusses the why or the cause of a death as well as the manner of the death.

The cause of death is the specific injury or disease that leads to death.
The manner of death is the determination of how the injury or disease leads to death. There are five manners of death (natural, accident, suicide, homicide, and undetermined).

Let's blend those insights with the other two definitions at the beginning of this chapter.

- The destruction or permanent end of something
- A damaging or destructive state of affairs

A marriage dies when it is injured or in response to something that has infected it, when it suffers damage that causes it to permanently and irreparably end.

How important it is for us to be clear about this. Beyond the usual responses to loss, we need to realize that a marriage that has ended has been damaged. The relationship has not been healthy. The union's damage and poor health were allowed to fester beyond curing and finally die.

Recognizing that is necessary to recover and heal. Moving out of the fog and heaviness of loss starts with the realization that what has happened is beyond changing. The past is simply the past.

The healing process, however, also requires us to look honestly at the manner of the death. We should not avoid an honest and often painful look at what brought the marriage to that point. We must grapple with what injury or unhealthiness of the marriage led to its death. The life of the relationship did not just suddenly disappear.

This part of the healing requires reflection. Undoubtedly, you will reflect on how the relationship started: the way you met, the dating, and the experience of love and your marriage ceremony. Look back at the events in your lives and search for those moments when the relationship changed. And it will! But did those changes bring you together or cause some measure of differences that were left unresolved? Did the gaps grow wider, the warmth grow cooler? How did you respond? How did your spouse respond?

Remember, the past is the past. You cannot change it.

But if you can be open and clear about the way the relationship became damaged and unhealthy, you will be better equipped to avoid the hurts and experiences of the past being repeated in any relationships in the future.

Now, let's look a little closer at the medical examiner's statements about the manner of death.

"The manner of death is the determination of how the injury or disease leads to death. There are five manners of death (natural, accident, suicide, homicide, and undetermined)."

Natural death obviously occurs when a spouse dies, bringing the marriage relationship to an end, even though the soul tie lingers.

Accidental death, according to USLegal.com[2], is defined as referring to "a death resulting from an unusual event that was unanticipated by everyone involved. It should not be intended, expected, or foreseeable,".

"I didn't mean to do that. It was an accident!" I imagine we have all said that, more than once. I remember a time early in my marriage when that was how I responded when I realized I had done something that really bothered my wife.

My wife and I had social circles filled with friends before we were married. Some of those circles overlapped. When we were around some of my former friends, I enjoyed having a good time, not realizing everybody there didn't know my wife, and I was not introducing her when I should.

I wasn't intentionally disregarding my wife. But I was not conscious of how much she felt like an outsider. She already had some self-esteem issues from her past that she had overcome, so when I was not thinking of her in those get-togethers, she really felt hurt.

This caused a bit of unrest in the Smith house! Well, to be honest, it grew into a powder keg, ready to explode!

We talked about it a lot and resolved the problem. I promised to be more considerate of my wife in these situations. And it didn't matter whether I thought they already knew her; I would introduce her, anyway.

Going through that experience was challenging and enlightening. I didn't realize it was happening. It was unintentional, an accident; but it was damaging my wife and infecting our marriage. Left to fester, this could have been the kind of thing that could kill the marriage altogether.

When we unintentionally do things that traumatize our union, the key to healing is to address the trauma that has been caused, i.e., operate on it, then come up with a decisive plan for recovery.

Suicide. Merriam-Webster defines suicide

as the act or an instance of taking one's own life voluntarily and intentionally.

Whether intentional or not, it is easy for some of us to end up killing the life we have together, simply by not developing a bond that includes planning for the future.

I am not proud of it, but I have been married three times. Each time I got married, I was optimistic for the future and visions of beautiful things coming our way. There was so much we weren't going to overcome together. Our love was strong and unbreakable.

But I walked into each marriage with no thought about a plan for our future as a couple or the families we were merging.

Benjamin Franklin once said, "If you fail to plan, you are planning to fail!"

Failing to plan and share a purpose as a couple is a formula for marital suicide. How can we expect these beautiful hopes and dreams to be anything more than fairy tales if we aren't actively pursuing the life we want together? How do we know what life is now and what it will be in the future if we don't sit down and set goals?

My wife and I really want to have a healthy and happy home. We don't enjoy arguing, fussing, and tension between us. And when any of those things show up, we have to resolve them, or they will potentially hurt our relationship.

When I failed to introduce my wife to my friends, unintentionally assuming she probably already knew them, she felt very uncomfortable and hurt. I realized I need to be aware of any areas in which she is sensitive. I am responsible for respecting those feelings and doing what I must to avoid causing her any discomfort.

We all have things we are sensitive about, not because we are weak, but just because we are human beings with feelings. Each of us needs to take care not to cause the other any undue pain.

A friend of mine told me of his own experience with this. He had taken his fiancée to his church, and some friends sat on the same pew with him as usual. The person next to him was a lady about his age, and when the music began, he realized she did not have a chorus sheet. He shared his sheet with her.

The fiancée was not happy about that. To her, he was disrespecting her by paying attention to his attractive friend. Was it inadvertent? Yes, but it was also dumb. He realized he needed to avoid any action that his fiancée could misinterpret. She needed to sense that she was his priority.

He could have tried to explain his point of view to her, and even try to tell her not to be so thin-skinned; but wisely, he apologized and realized that he needed to act in ways that communicated to her that their new relationship meant more than other relationships.

We create marital suicide when we don't consider how our actions will be understood by our spouses. My friend needed to be aware of how this situation would look to his fiancée. And had he failed to respond lovingly to her that day, a fuse could have been lit that could have destroyed their relationship. Failure to put your spouse's welfare and needs ahead of your own is a path that can lead to marital suicide.

Homicide is defined as the deliberate and unlawful killing of one person by another; murder. A significant cause of killing a marriage comes from allowing entities outside of your union to damage the health of your marriage. Over time, those outside influences, left unchecked, can kill your marriage.

Often, marital homicides happen because we allow people too much access to our marriages, especially close friends and family.

There's no better hitman in marriage than an unhappy family member. They begin by talking about how your spouse should do such-and-such like daddy used to do it. Then, they graduate to how your spouse isn't doing this or that. They are planting seeds. You trust them. So, what they're saying must be right.

Then, one day, your spouse does what he or she usually does, and suddenly, "I've been dealing with this for way too long." Everything that they've been planting has surfaced. And the person who you loved is now the focus of THEIR pain!

When my mom and dad got married, some people hated my mom. They treated her like garbage every chance that they had. They scandalized her. Talked down to her and were just mean people. This went on for years!

There were many times that I overheard my parents arguing about how my mom was being treated. Many nights, I heard her crying out to God in her bedroom, asking for relief from the stress she was feeling from this abuse.

This happened so long that those treating her poorly realized they wouldn't break her down by attacking her. They started attacking me.

The rest of the children could play. But I had to go sit down. They bought push-ups and bomb-pops for all the children. But since they didn't have enough money, I had to eat whatever leftover ice cream they had in the freezer.

They were deliberately trying to break up my parents' marriage, and I hated them for it.

So much energy was put into trying to

destroy my mom that they didn't see they were strengthening her.

We don't have to allow marital homicide to happen. Sometimes, all that we need to do is weather the allegations, complaints, and the barrage of misinformation. Liars and deceivers will get what they deserve. The Law of Reaping and Sowing (or as some call it, Karma) will always come back to those who have visited it on others.

Unfortunately, not everyone is as secure as my mom. Many give up on marriage because their families or close friends don't think that their spouse is good enough for them.

When I proposed to my wife, it was a total surprise for all of us, including me!

We were longtime friends. We enjoyed each other's company. I could see her as the future Mrs. Smith, and so I popped the question.

Unfortunately, the response from those closest to my wife was bewilderment, disgust, and questioning what she was thinking. The calls got so bad on the day that I proposed that I caught her crying and confused, wondering about her decision to say yes.

Then she spoke to her father, and it no longer mattered what everyone else was saying. He was so excited that his baby was getting married that he rejoiced and cried so hard that we started crying with him! He cried and proclaimed his love for God so much that he hung up without asking whether she had accepted my proposal!

Don't fall prey to the homicidal maniacs out there.

Many people commit marital homicide just because their own life isn't what they wanted, and misery loves company. They bond on the mutual sense of being treated unfairly, the belief that everybody else is against them, that they get no breaks, and everybody else gets a break but them. Their relationship is built on mutual misery. And that foundation is weak. Two miserable people become one miserable union.

And then the cause of some marriages is simply said to be "undetermined." Those looking on seem to have no clue, and often

ESTABLISHING GLORY 3

the two whose bond has been broken seem equally at a loss to explain it. The general fallback expressions are "irreconcilable differences" or "things just didn't work out."

What is irreconcilable or what did not work out simply means that neither of the spouses put the work in to reconcile or work at their differences. One or both just wimped out. Life got hard, and they got their coats and, in their self-focused stubbornness, marched off with a vague idea that the next relationship will be the "right one." But as the old adage says, "wherever they go, they take themselves with them."

So, while our relationship is filled with smiles and daisies, we should be focused on getting to know the person sitting across the table from us. What are his or her strengths? Where does he or she need to grow, and what can we do to build him or her up? And while we are at it, it would be wise to be brutally honest about our own strengths and weaknesses. This kind of honesty will either lead you to fight for your marriage or the idea of fight will too easily be replaced by the thoughts of flight.

A threat to our marriage comes from the twisted culture of our times. Our values have been infected with a blinding desire for pleasure. People try to medicate themselves with accumulating things, confusing want with need. They turn to destructive behaviors that lead to damage and even destroy their relationship in a mutual addiction to abandoning social and moral boundaries.

Two areas of this cultural shift that are dangerously addictive. The first of these is the belief that more money and power will fix anything. Greed governs behavior that justifies a lack of ethics and even lawlessness that fosters the idea that anything we want is ours to get or take any way we can.

Couples who embrace this idea destroy their marriages because their self-centeredness will inevitably be the seed of dividing them. Left unchecked, the marriage will not survive.

The second cultural shift is the preoccupation with the deterioration and abandonment of sexual boundaries. I include this topic because the entertainment and marketing worlds have inundated our culture with an increasing and intentional redefining of sexuality, casting off any traditional boundaries.

Pornography is now commonly used and labeled as a private matter that is victimless. Many couples now make use of pornography as a shared experience. Their appetites for this so-called "freedom from restraints" drive them to what they may call "mutual pleasure," but in reality, it drives them apart into a world of their individual desires rather than mutual welfare.

A spouse may seek more "exciting pleasure" in a relationship outside of his or her marriage. Or one spouse may suggest sharing sex with someone else or another couple, and the appeal of pleasure leads them to set aside any kind of reluctance.

This path leads to devaluing each other and an addiction that will inevitably cheapen their relationship and drive them to disregard every other value in preference to their own. And this abandons the anchor of self-worth.

Such deviation from the moral foundation of valuing each other and mutual respect is mutual suicide waiting to happen.

Marital suicide results from mutually abandoning the promise to love and cherish each other and only each other as long as you live. When a marriage has lost the bond of being "as one," there is the risk of damage and relational illness that becomes irreversible.

❧ 9 ☙
ACCORDING TO GOD'S HOLY ORDINANCE

The institution of marriage isn't just another trend or fad that can be updated to suit the will and whim of a generation. It is an established covenant between a man and a woman designated, created, and ordained by God.

The social norm of our day applauds the rejection of tradition and traditional values. We are encouraged to make our own way, to follow a path of our own choosing, one that is free from the restraints of outdated thinking. The problem is that we don't have anything to replace it, except the notion that every person's set of values is as legitimate as anyone else's.

The heart and will of each person is left to define what life should look like for them. Being social beings, however, the natural tendency is to advocate for that view of reality and try to impress others to join you. And in today's social and moral climate, there seems to be an unquenchable desire for the "new" way of thinking.

This mindset takes a toll on marriage.

The definition of marriage has been hijacked by a culture that no longer acknowledges the authority of God and, for all practical purposes, denies His existence entirely. So, the idea of marriage as a "holy ordinance" has no meaning.

Marriage has become a relationship of convenience, and when it is no longer convenient or serves the self-interest of one or both spouses, they move on. In fact, marriage is even defined as an inconvenience and unnecessary.

The cultural definition has changed beyond the union of a man and a woman.

ESTABLISHING GLORY 3

Love itself has been redefined to legitimize same sex "marriages." The Biblical idea of marriage is now being ignored.

Having turned away from God and the values that have held civilization together, the objections to same-sex relationships are called divisive and hate-filled. The cultural drift now includes legitimizing gay marriage by churches who have replaced faithfulness to Truth with the social doctrine of inclusion. Their choice is a twisted declaration that God places His seal of approval on that union.

The Bible is noticeably clear about homosexuality. Leviticus 18:22 NKJV says, *"You shall not lie with a male as with a woman. It is an abomination."* And it is equally abominable to act in the name of God in total rejection of His word.

The churches that set aside what God has declared and assert that following Him is about being inclusive have lost their way. Under the guise of spreading love, they mirror political and social correctness as if that is compatible with God's views. They don the garments of darkened thinking instead of being clothed in God's likeness. Second Timothy 3:5 KJV speaks of *"Having a form of godliness, but denying the power thereof: from such turn away."* The human distortion of truth takes the form of godliness but is empty of the power of true godliness.

What power do we have when we call ungodliness as if it were godliness? When we no longer recognize the God who authors holiness, the words "God's holy ordinance" no longer have meaning. Since Hebrews 12:14 NIV clearly declares that *"without holiness no one will see the Lord,"* the idea of ungodliness forfeits any measure of His likeness and blinds us from recognizing God or His truth. The fact that our society has accepted and promotes the LGBTQ+ lifestyle doesn't mean that it's right.

I know and have friends who have chosen this lifestyle. The discussion this far is not a form of bashing them. Any act to defy God's directives or redefine them for convenience is the definition of sin, and sin comes in many forms. As a Christian, I am to value every person just as God does, but I can no more endorse homosexuality than I can any other sin. As God grieves at sinfulness, we, as His children, also have to grieve, but the sin itself must remain offensive. Marriage is by His directives as a holy ordinance or a law established by His grace.

God Himself established the first marriage in Genesis 2 when He brought together the man and the woman He had made in His own likeness. Adam's response to her is classic. Genesis 2:23 MSG states, *"Finally! Bone of my bone, flesh of my flesh! Name her Woman for she was made from Man."* He immediately claimed her and named her.

When a marriage takes place between a man and a woman who embrace the faithfulness those vows declare, God honors that union. Even for those who are not believers, the choice to walk in faithfulness to each other is one He favors.

God said in His act of creation that man was not to live alone, so in Proverbs 18:22 NIV, He makes His view quite clear: *"He who finds a wife finds what is good and receives favor from the LORD."* To those who seek to make their relationship one that reflects His likeness, He adds in Proverbs 10:22, *"The blessing of the Lord, it maketh rich, and he addeth no sorrow with it."* God's plan for marriage is that it is to bring us security, stability, and partnership. Those are the things that define the richness He spoke of in that verse.

The security of marriage comes from our mutual trust. A marriage that reflects God's design is one in which both spouses have each other's backs. They would never intentionally hurt each other. We have each other's back.

The stability of marriage is evidence of a holy ordinance. God, who does not change, shares, and as we seek His likeness, we can experience the strength of stability. Each spouse can sense that no matter what comes their way, they are loved, and the commitment of that love is strong. Unlike the roller coaster rides other friendships take us through, they know they can rely on their spouse.

The likeness of God is also seen in the partnership of marriage. Our commitment to be life-mates, to be each other's ride or die. Together, it's us against the world.

These are just a few of the things that make marital blessings rich!

God declares that society is to hold the institution of marriage as sacred.

> *"Marriage is to be held in honor among all [that is, regarded as something of great value], and the marriage bed undefiled [by immorality or by any sexual sin]; for God will judge the sexually immoral and adulterous,"*
>
> — (HEBREWS 13:4 AMP).

The wording of that verse in The Message MSG expresses a parallel between honoring marriage and guarding the sacredness of sexual intimacy between a wife and husband. God draws a firm line against casual and illicit sex.

A marriage lived as a holy ordinance tells us that the sexual union of marriage is to be respected and guarded. That part of the relationship is to be secure and undefiled.

God made us to be intimate, and that intimacy is to be enjoyed within the boundaries of the sacredness of marriage. It is also how we can bear children, extensions of our sacred bond.

In short, the bond we share as a couple is with the God who ordained the institution of marriage. For those who may not marry, and if they have the spiritual giftedness of celibacy, they can enjoy their bond with the Lord. But the Apostle Paul notes in 1 Corinthians 7:2 ESV that if someone's relationship with God is distracted by the temptation of sexual immorality, it is better for them to marry and adds that *"each man should have his own wife and each woman her own husband."* While sexuality is normal, it is not to be misused or experienced outside the bonds of marriage. The married couple is to carefully guard that relationship because anything that intrudes or defiles it violates His design for a man and a woman to be one. They are to belong solely to each other as a holy union.

ESTABLISHING GLORY 3

As we discussed in the previous chapter, the world we live in today can easily infect us with a distorted image of sex and love. Those who seek to live in holy matrimony must never allow their bond to include any practice that defiles the union. Multiple partners, the world's enticement to persuade you to respond to such deviancies as "open marriage," together or separately, defiles what God designed for us and allows the enemy to gain a foothold that can lead to the destruction of the marriage.

Again, the Apostle Paul speaks clearly to this matter in 1 Corinthians 7:

> *Sexual drives are powerful, but marriage is strong enough to contain them and provide a balanced and fulfilling sexual life in a world of sexual disorder.*

He then adds,
"*The marriage bed must be a place of mutuality —the husband seeking to satisfy his wife, the wife*

seeking to satisfy her husband. Marriage is not a place to "stand up for your rights." Marriage is a decision to serve the other, whether in bed or out (1 Corinthians 7:2-6 MSG).

Notice that we are to serve each other. This is a term that contains the idea of ministry. The marriage relationship is a sacred ministry dedicated to each other. Our whole relationship is one of meeting the needs of each other "in bed or out." Paul's expression, translated here as "serving" each other, is not to be confused with the twisted cultural use of that term. This is how your intimacy responds to God's plan for us to be one.

Marriage is an image of God's commitment to the Church. Physical intimacy responds to each other's natural desire to be complete. Yet, there is a spiritual intimacy with God that forever completes us. Our willingness to be selfless and passionate about each other's desire to be complete is a human experience that pales in comparison to the selflessness of Christ, whose focus was on our needs rather than His own. As with the Lord, our bond is a connection of our entire self, mind, body, and soul.

But Paul is not finished with his instruction. In 1 Corinthians 7:5, he says:

> *"Do not deprive each other [of marital rights], except perhaps by mutual consent for a time, so that you may devote yourselves [unhindered] to prayer, but come together again so that Satan will not tempt you [to sin] because of your lack of self-control."*

The marriage relationship, this ordinance from God, is to be for mutual benefit. The role of husband and wife is not to be centered on each other only part of the time. We are to meet each other's needs in all aspects of our relationship, including the sexual bond.

However, we are not to allow natural desires to stand in the way of our spiritual roles. A couple living in a holy relationship must recognize that there are times when spiritual purposes take precedence over physical desires.

In the Bible, physical intimacy is expressed as "knowing": Adam "knew" his wife, for example. Mary, the mother of Jesus, had not "known" Joseph until after the birth of Jesus. There is a real sense that intimacy, sexual or otherwise, is a time of unmasking and allowing ourselves to be vulnerable. We realize the value of our spouse. We discover nuances of who they are or new measures of what we already value in each other.

Paul's word in 1 Corinthians 7:5 points to physical intimacy, but the principle is that we are not to withhold intimacy from each other. We are to be vulnerable and transparent. Failing to experience mutual intimacy denies the other the privilege of growing closer with us and us to them. As God desires to reveal Himself to us and allow us to grow in our bond with Him, we should reflect the same desire to be transparent in our relationship.

A husband and wife who withhold intimacy will eventually become strangers.

ESTABLISHING GLORY 3

They grow apart rather than experience growing strength as one.

Paul, of course, points out that a lack of physical intimacy opens the door to temptation. The enemy will put someone in your path as an invitation to satisfy that desire. The same is true of intimacy of any kind. In its absence, the heart is tempted to seek it somewhere else.

The ministry of marriage is a sacred trust. Jesus said in Matthew 6:22, *"seek ye first the kingdom of God, and his righteousness."* That is the key to the bond you will have with Him, but it will also ensure that earthly bonds will be viewed through the same lens. This is the key to experiencing the other blessings of God, including a healthy relationship with your spouse.

In Ephesians 5:22-24 MSG, we find that husbands and wives are to experience mutual submission:

> *Wives, understand and support your husbands in ways that show your support for Christ. The*

> *husband provides leadership to his wife the way Christ does to his church, not by domineering but by cherishing. So just as the church submits to Christ as he exercises such leadership, wives should likewise submit to their husbands.*

The key to "understanding and supporting" is submitting. If you are not willing to submit, you are choosing to stay self-focused instead of understanding your spouse and affirming his or her value.

Then, for the husbands:

> *Husbands, go all out in your love for your wives, exactly as Christ did for the church—a love marked by giving, not getting. Christ's love makes the church whole. His words evoke her beauty. Everything he does and says brings the best out of her, dressing her in dazzling*

> *white silk, radiant with holiness. And that is how husbands ought to love their wives. They're really doing themselves a favor—since they're already "one" in marriage.*

The instructions to husbands also point out a posture of submission to the needs of their wives. The husband is to make his wife's need for support, strength, and growth, especially her spiritual growth, his priority in the same way Christ gave Himself for the Church. A husband's love is sacrificial.

The spiritual posture of love is one of giving of yourself. The old claim that marriage is a 50-50 proposition is not Biblical. The formula for a successful marriage relationship is 100-100. Each gives him or herself completely to support and strengthen each other. And in that way, they are making themselves stronger and healthier.

God's desire for marriage is that we provide an earthly example that reminds people of Christ's relationship with His Church.

God's directive to Adam and Eve was to take possession of what He had created. They were to be fruitful and multiplying; because caring for His creation included, by His design, the role of filling the earth by reproduction.

The creative nature of God is evidenced in the nature and instincts of the creation. And Adam and Eve, made explicitly in His likeness, were to be "fruitful" and fill the earth with offspring, who also would bear His likeness.

Just as God made us individually to be reflections of Him, in the same way His holy ordinance of marriage is to reflect His relationship with us as well. This provides a model of love that invites others to want their relationship to be healthy and whole.

Again, using the thought of reproduction, great marriages reproduce great marriages!

I was blessed to have a childhood in which both of my parents were in the home. I saw the challenges and triumphs of marriage. I experienced the greatness of their relationship, and it made me want to have a great marriage someday. My goal was to follow my parents' example.

Some who will read this book may not have had that kind of experience growing up. And if you're still reading, you apparently want to experience something better than what was modeled for you. And let me assure you, that is not beyond reach.

The key is connecting with people and marriages that are successful, and more specifically, those marriage relationships that are grounded in God's holy ordinance. Learn from them. Glean from their experiences with those qualities that you want to have in your own life. This way, you can reproduce what you see in them.

Begin with the holy ordinance that God designed marriage to be, and your life together will be fruitful models for others as well.

The health of society depends on the spiritual health of the family.

10

AND THERETO I PLEDGE MYSELF TO YOU

At the conclusion of the marriage vows, an exchange takes place. The wording may vary in different versions of the vows, but it is stated, the bride and groom pledge themselves to each other.

According to Merriam-Webster, these are the definitions of the word pledge:

- a bailment of a chattel as security for a debt or other obligation without involving the transfer of title

- the state of being held as security or a guaranty
- a token, sign, or earnest of something else
- a gage of battle
- a toast
- a binding promise or agreement to do or forbear

At one time, when a man wanted to take a bride, he or his family had to pay what was called a bride price, sometimes called a bride service, to formalize and legitimize a traditional marriage, and it also allowed that marriage to be held in a church or civil service. The union was considered invalid if the bride price wasn't paid in full at the time of the marriage or at least paid within the agreed time required.

Conversely, in many cultures, the bride would bring a dowry into marriage as an offering to the groom and his family. The dowry could be money, land, or any other asset in exchange for marriage. Just as the purpose of the bride price is not to "purchase" a bride, the dowry is not the price to secure a husband, but both are expressions of respect for the family and a demonstration of how much the bride or groom is valued. And in both cases, these exchanges are a guarantee against divorce.

At least in the United States of America, giving a literal bride price or dowry became illegal as time passed. However, the exchange of worth still takes place when a bride's family traditionally covers the cost of the wedding. The groom is expected to take care of rehearsal dinners and honeymoon expenses.

But in terms of the vows, there was still a need to make an exchange during the marriage ceremony. Then enters the "troth."

"Troth" is an archaic word with two basic definitions:

1. faith or loyalty when pledged in a solemn agreement or undertaking, and
2. truth. These two definitions point in the same direction. A vow to live truthfully certainly includes loyalty

and fidelity. A lady once said, "I don't trust women." Then, she continued to describe how other women have made advances toward her husband, where he works.

Even though he had a wedding ring, one lady left her phone number on his final receipt. Another woman gave him her Snapchat account and asked him to snap with her later that night.

Her husband did not respond to either suggestion. He was committed to his vow to love and cherish his wife. But it occurred to me that this is not about trusting other people but about having confidence and trust in your spouse.

The pledge in our vows is a commitment to a covenant. It is a pledge by both the bride and the groom to a relationship of faithfulness and selflessness.

A pledge or covenant is only as binding as the person making it. This is a covenant relationship, a kind of "contract" to which both parties declare their commitment that will bind them to each other. This covenant is about faithfully loving and caring for each other's needs, tending to their growth and care, and being the source of their strength. These words promise to address the other's desires and place their needs even above yours.

Sadly, that sense of covenant in our culture seems to have become as archaic as the word "troth." Almost half of all marriages in our country end in divorce. We have lost the genuine sense that covenant is more than words. It is a commitment that requires deliberate choices to follow. You have to work to have a committed relationship.

This kind of relationship requires work because the enemy will make every effort to derail us. He knows we are not blind and will use any means to entice us. The handsome man or beautiful lady can become his bait.

In such moments, I have had to reaffirm my vow of commitment to my wife. My life has changed, and I am in a covenant relationship with her.

When we waver in our commitment, that

choice will have a penalty. Back in another era, that would have required returning a bride price or a dowry. Try marrying someone and receiving 100 acres of land just to give the land back because you don't want to be married anymore!

Today, the price is set by legal requirements and is increasingly costly. The expected 50-50 split often becomes a bit more lopsided than that. While joking about getting a divorce, Eddie Murphy once said, "I've never met a woman who was worth half."

As someone who has been divorced, it isn't just about half of my "stuff." When our pledge and commitment are broken, it costs me a part of myself. I'm not the same person I was before I got married.

When we look at the pledge, we must also look at whom the promise is being given to. Most of us only look at our beautiful, blushing bride or the handsome, caring groom in front of us. But there's much more happening at that moment. The covenant we are sealing is before "God and these witnesses"!

As a witness to the pledge, we become a party to the promise.

There was a time when people would help couples stay together! The older men would help the younger guys with words of wisdom. And the older women would guide the younger ladies.

This support from the community helped build stronger marriages because the witnesses to the marriage took stock in the union's outcome.

God's approval of marriage and His witness give power to the seriousness of this commitment. We say honoring God's union isn't essential when we break the covenant.

We are dishonoring God!

Therefore, marriage shouldn't be entered into lightly.

No one ever said that getting and staying married was an easy venture. No matter who you are or who you are married to, there will be days that are more challenging than others. And even moments when you may feel you don't want to be married at all.

The key is that marriage is worth it!

Whether you have read this book as part of your pre-marital counseling or you've been married to your bride for 90 years, marriage is a noble institution! It requires work. But the benefits of the work far outweigh any challenges you'll face!

On the final page of this book, I have included a special prayer entitled "Prayer for Married Couples." May we embrace this as our own.

PRAYER FOR MARRIED COUPLES

— *Archdiocese of Baltimore, 1990* [1]

Lord God, we acknowledge your greatness
and our need for your grace in our marriage.

We thank you now for the gift you have given
us in each other,
this opportunity to love and be loved
completely.

We accept this beautiful challenge and ask
you to bless us.

May our love encourage us to grow to be
holier individuals,
bringing out the best in each other.

Following your example, Jesus, may we be
quick to forgive,
ready with a healing word or touch.

Teach us to speak to each other with charity
and honesty.

JACKIE SMITH, JR.

Help us avoid the temptation to take each other for granted.

Instead, remind us, day by day, to see each other as you see us.

May we be as patient with each other as you are with us.

May our love be generous,
reaching out beyond ourselves to all we meet.

We pray that they may meet you in us.

Let our life together be a light of hope to those who
fear that a total commitment is not possible today.

Faith gives us courage,
for we believe that the love that comes
from you is freeing and life-giving.

Lord, be a partner with us in our marriage;
with your help, it will be strong and enduring.

We rejoice that you have brought us together.

May we always be one in you.
Amen.

ENDNOTES

5. FOR RICHER, FOR POORER: BEYOND MONEY

1. https://www.focusonthefamily.com/marriage/ten-secrets-to-a-successful-marriage/

7. TO LOVE AND TO CHERISH

1. https://tolovehonorandvacuum.com/2014/05/breaking-soul-ties/
2. https://www.psychologytoday.com/us/blog/hide-and-seek/201606/these-are-the-7-types-love

8. TILL DEATH DO US PART

1. https://www.washoecounty.us/coroner/faq/difference_cause_and_manner_of_death.php
2. https://definitions.uslegal.com/a/accidental-death/

10. AND THERETO I PLEDGE MYSELF TO YOU

1. https://www.archbalt.org/marriage-family-life/prayer-married-couple/

ABOUT THE AUTHOR

Jackie Smith, Jr. is an African-American writer who grew up in Columbus, Ohio. Using his experiences as a technical trainer, business owner, professional musician, and licensed minister he penned, Establishing Glory, a faith-based self-help series.

His goal in life is to help people be their best which he does it by shining an unfiltered light on the challenges of his own life including faith, marriage, music, divorce, and parenting in the 2000s.

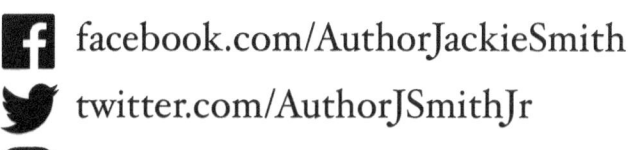

facebook.com/AuthorJackieSmith
twitter.com/AuthorJSmithJr
instagram.com/AuthorJackieSmith

ALSO BY JACKIE SMITH, JR.

Establishing Glory: The Praise and Worship Handbook (ISBN: 9781950719006)

Establishing Glory 2: The Relationship Handbook (ISBN: 9781950719037)

Sex After Divorce: Been There, Done That & Had The Orgasm To Prove It! (ISBN: 9781734087000)

www.ingramcontent.com/pod-product-compliance
Lightning Source LLC
Chambersburg PA
CBHW020139130526
44591CB00030B/150